PowerKids Readers:

MY SCHOOL™

Meet the Librarian

Elizabeth Vogel

The Rosen Publishing Group's
PowerKids Press
New York

Rosen Publishing would like to extend special thanks to Geneseo Elementary School and Kathy Booth

Published in 2002 by The Rosen Publishing Group, Inc.
29 East 21st Street, New York, NY 10010

First Edition

Book Design: Michael Donnellan

Photo Credits: All photos by Angela Booth.

Vogel, Elizabeth.
Meet the librarian / Elizabeth Vogel.— 1st ed.
     p. cm. — (My school)
Includes bibliographical references (p.   ) and index.
  ISBN 0-8239-6031-5 (lib. bdg.)
1. Librarians—Juvenile literature. 2. Libraries—Juvenile literature. [1. School librarians. 2. Librarians. 3. Libraries. 4. Occupations.] I. Title.
  Z665.5 .V64 2002
  020'.92—dc21

                                          2001000166

Manufactured in the United States of America

Contents

I am a librarian. I work with a lot of books.

You can find me in the school library. The library has books on many different topics.

When you visit, you can choose a book to read.

9

Sometimes I will read
a book out loud.

I will show you where to find your favorite stories.

13

Sometimes you need a special book for a report. I can use the computer to help you find your book.

Each book has its own place on the shelves. I can tell where a book belongs because of the numbers on its spine. The spine is here, on the side of a book.

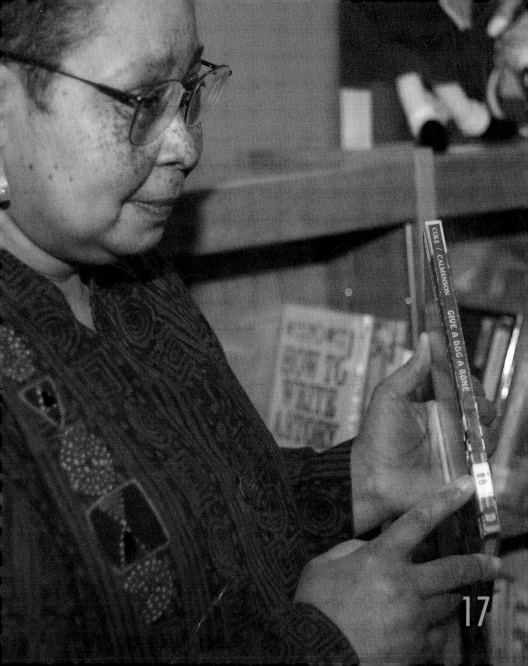

At the library, you can check out books. This means you can take them home and return them on another day. I'll show you how!

The library is a special place. I will always be here to help you when you visit the library.

Words to Know

computer

shelves

spine (of the book)

Here are more books to read about librarians:

A Day With a Librarian (Hard Work)
by Jan Kottke
Children's Press

Ms. Davison, Our Librarian (Our Neighborhood [New York, N.Y.])
by Alice K. Flanagan,
Children's Press

To learn more about librarians, check out this Web site:
www.ala.org

Index

Word Count: 152

Note to Librarians, Teachers, and Parents

PowerKids Readers are specially designed to help emergent and beginning readers build their skills in reading for information. Simple vocabulary and concepts are paired with stunning, detailed images from the natural world around them. Readers will respond to written language by linking meaning with their own everyday experiences and observations. Sentences are short and simple, employing a basic vocabulary of sight words, as well as new words that describe objects or processes that take place in the natural world. Large type, clean design, and photographs corresponding directly to the text all help children to decipher meaning. Features such as a contents page, picture glossary, and index help children get the most out of PowerKids Readers. They also introduce children to the basic elements of a book, which they will encounter in their future reading experiences. Lists of related books and Web sites encourage kids to explore other sources and to continue the process of learning.